JERMYN STREET THEATRE

Infamous

by April De Angelis

T0322548

First performed at Jermyn Street Theatre, London,
from 7 September – 7 October 2023.

cast

Emma Hamilton (1815) / Mrs Cadogan	**CAROLINE QUENTIN**
Emma Hamilton (1798) / Horatia Nelson	**ROSE QUENTIN**
Vincenzo / Jacques Fournier	**RIAD RICHIE**

creative team

Writer	**APRIL DE ANGELIS**
Director	**MICHAEL OAKLEY**
Designer	**FOTINI DIMOU**
Lighting Designer	**CHRISTOPHER NAIRNE**
Composer and Sound Designer	**BETH DUKE**
Choreographer	**MANDY DEMETRIOU**
Assistant Director	**BRIGITTE ADELA**
Dramaturg	**CHARLOTTE THOMPSON**
Italian Language Consultant	**GABRIELE UBOLDI**
Production Manager	**LUCY MEWIS-MCKERROW**
Stage Manager	**SUMMER KEELING**
Assistant Stage Manager	**MORGAN TOOLE**
Photographers	**HUGO GLENDINNING**
	STEVE GREGSON
PR	**DAVID BURNS**
Executive Producer	**DAVID DOYLE**

Special thanks to Joan Hughes, Tom Littler, Ellie Williams, and Hackney Showroom.

cast

Caroline Quentin Emma Hamilton (1815) / Mrs Cadogan

Theatre includes: *Mrs Warren's Profession* (Theatre Royal Bath/UK Tour); *Jack Absolute Flies Again*, *The London Cuckolds* (National Theatre); *The Provoked Wife* (Royal Shakespeare Company); *Me and My Girl* (Chichester Festival Theatre); *The Hypocrite* (Hull Truck/Royal Shakespeare Company); *The Life and Times of Fanny Hill* (Bristol Old Vic); *Relative Values* (Theatre Royal Bath); *Oh What A Lovely War!* (Theatre Royal Stratford East); *Terrible Advice* (Menier Chocolate Factory); *Life After Scandal* (Hampstead Theatre).

Television includes: *The Lazarus Project* (Sky); *Life Begins*, *Men Behaving Badly*, *Blue Murder* (ITV); *Jonathan Creek*, *The Other One*, *Life of Riley*, *Kiss Me Kate* (BBC); *Bridgerton*, *Dickensian* (Netflix).

Film includes: *Love Me Tinder*; *Miss Willoughby and the Haunted Bookshop*.

Rose Quentin Emma Hamilton (1798) / Horatia Nelson

Theatre includes: *Mrs. Warren's Profession* (Theatre Royal Bath/UK Tour); *The Legend of Sleepy Hollow* (UK Tour).

Television includes: *Doc Martin* (ITV); *Doctors* (BBC); *Little Crackers* (Sky).

Film includes: *York Witches' Society*.

Riad Richie Vincenzo / Jacques Fournier

Theatre includes: *Of Mice and Men* (Birmingham Rep/UK Tour); *Tartuffe* (Birmingham Rep/Royal Shakespeare Company); *The Marlowe Session* (The Malthouse); *Jabala and the Jinn* (Turtle Key Arts); *The Comedy of Errors*, *The Whip*, *A Museum in Baghdad*, *Timon of Athens*, *Tartuffe*, *Tamburlaine* (Royal Shakespeare Company); *A Midsummer Night's Dream* (Shakespeare in the Squares); *The Show in which Hopefully Nothing Happens* (Unicorn Theatre/Theatre Artemis); *Macbeth*, *Romeo and Juliet*, *Mark and the Marked*, *The Merchant of Venice*, *Frankenstein*, *The Passenger* (Box Clever); *The Changeling*, *LOL* (Clifftown Theatre).

Film includes: *Said in Passing* (Short); *iBoy*; *The Last Amendment* (Short); *The Gates of Vanity*; *The Guardians* (Short); *Top Dog*; *Cinderella*; *Cluedo* (Short).

creative team

April De Angelis Writer

Theatre includes: *Kerry Jackson* (National Theatre); *Saving Grace* (Riverside Studios); *Gin Craze!* (Royal & Derngate Northampton); *My Brilliant Friend* (Rose Theatre Kingston/National Theatre); *The Village* (Theatre Royal Stratford East); *Frankenstein* (Royal Exchange Manchester); *Gastronauts* (Royal Court Theatre Upstairs); *Jumpy* (Royal Court/Duke of York's Theatre/Southbank Theatre, Melbourne/Sydney Opera House); *Wuthering Heights* (Birmingham Rep); *Wild East* (Royal Court/Young Vic); *A Laughing Matter* (Out of Joint/National Theatre); *A Warwickshire Testimony* (Royal Shakespeare Company); *The Positive Hour* (Out of Joint/Hampstead Theatre); *Playhouse Creatures* (Old Vic/Chichester Festival Theatre); *The Life and Times of Fanny Hill* (Red Shift/The Old Fire Station, Oxford/Bristol Old Vic); *Flight* (Glyndebourne Opera).

Television includes: *Unprecedented*, *House Party* (BBC Four); *Aristophanes* (Bandung Productions/Channel 4). She is currently developing a television series (Drama Republic/Channel 4) based on her stage play *Jumpy*.

Opera includes: *The Silent Twins*, *Pig*, *Greed* (Almeida Theatre); *Die Fledermaus* (English National Opera).

Radio includes: *Life in the Tomb* (BBC Radio 3); *Sweet Dreams*, *I Leap Over the Wall*, *Cash Cows*, *Peyton Place* (BBC Radio); *The Outlander* (Radio 5); *Visitants* (Radio 4).

Michael Oakley Director

For Jermyn Street Theatre: *About Leo*.

Theatre includes: *Wilderness* (LAMDA); *Gin Craze!* (Royal & Derngate Northampton); *Romeo and Juliet*, *Much Ado About Nothing (*PSwDB, Shakespeare's Globe); *Wuthering Heights* (Lamplighter); *NOF*CKSGIVEN* (VAULT Festival); *Private Lives*, *As You Like It* (Oxford Shakespeare Company); *William Wordsworth* (Theatre by the Lake/English Touring Theatre); *A Lovely Sunday for Creve Coeur* (Coronet); *The Invisible* (Bush Theatre); *The Life and Times of Fanny Hill* (Bristol Old Vic/Lamplighter); *Variation on a Theme* (Finborough Theatre); *Playhouse Creatures* (Chichester Festival Theatre); *The Changeling* (Southwark Playhouse); *Edward II* (Battersea Arts Centre); *Citysong*, *The Seagull*, *The Threepenny Opera*, *All My Sons*, *The Country Wife* (East 15 Acting School); *Julius Caesar*, *Cymbeline* (Liverpool Institute for Performing Arts).

Michael was Trainee Director in Residence at Chichester Festival Theatre and a recipient of the prestigious JMK Award for young directors.

Fotini Dimou Designer

Film and television includes (as costume designer): *Smyrna* (Tanweer Productions); *The Children Act*; *King Lear, Man and Boy* (BBC Films); *The Dresser* (Playground Entertainment); *Skin; Ripley's Game* (Cattleya); *The Browning Version* (Paramount Pictures).

Fotini has worked extensively in theatre, opera and dance for the Royal Shakespeare Company, the National Theatre, Regent's Park Open Air Theatre, London's West End, Theatre Royal Bath, and Chichester Festival Theatre. For opera, she has designed for the Royal Opera House, English National Opera, Opera North, and abroad at the New York Metropolitan opera, Teatro alla Scala in Milano and in the Festispielhaus Baden-Baden. She won a BAFTA for her work on *The Dresser* and was nominated for a Royal Television Society Craft and Design Award for her work on *King Lear*. This is her fourth collaboration with Michael Oakley.

Christopher Nairne Lighting Designer

For Jermyn Street Theatre: *The Kissing-Dance, Anyone Can Whistle*.

Theatre includes: *Groan Ups* (West End/UK tour); *Tom Fool, Mayfly* (Orange Tree Theatre); *Jeeves and Wooster in Perfect Nonsense, The Last Temptation of Boris Johnson* (UK Tour); *Suzy Storck* (Gate Theatre/France Tour); *Keep on Walking Federico* (UK Tour/Theatre Lliure, Barcelona); *Chasing Bono, Tumulus* (Soho Theatre); *The Legend of Sleepy Hollow, The Beautiful Game*, A *Little Princess* (The Other Palace); *Jerusalem* (Watermill Theatre); *Speech and Debate, BU21* (Trafalgar Studios); *This Beautiful Future* (The Yard Theatre); *Lionboy* (World Tour).

Opera includes: *L'Agrippina* (Barber); *Madame Butterfly, Jephtha, Macbeth* (Iford Arts); *Belshazzar* (Trinity Laban Conservatoire); *Vivienne* (Royal Opera House); *La Bohème* (OperaUpClose).

christophernairne.co.uk

Beth Duke Composer and Sound Designer

Theatre includes: *Retrograde* (Kiln Theatre); *The Suspicions of Mr Whicher* (Watermill Theatre); *Strategic Love Play* (Belgrade Theatre/UK Tour); *The Trial of Josie K* (Unicorn Theatre); *Akedah* (Hampstead Theatre); *Beauty and the Beast* (Mercury Colchester); *Amma VR Experience* (Tara Theatre); *Death Drop: Back in the Habit* (Garrick Theatre/UK Tour); *A Single Man* (Park Theatre); *The Importance of Being Earnest* (English Touring Theatre); *Bridgerton* (Secret Cinema); *Mad House* (Ambassador's Theatre); *Mog the Forgetful Cat* (Royal & Derngate Northampton/Old Vic); *Robin Hood* (Bristol Old Vic); *Death Drop* (Garrick Theatre/Criterion Theatre/UK Tour); *J'Ouvert* (Harold Pinter Theatre/BBC); *One Jewish Boy* (Trafalgar Studios/West End/UK Tour); *Typical Girls* (Sheffield Crucible); *Scenes with Girls, Living Newspaper* (Royal Court); *Isla* (Theatre Clwyd); *Tuck Shop* (Garrick Theatre); *Patricia Gets Ready* (Pleasance/UK Tour); *Gentlemen, Pipeline*; *A Fantastic Bohemian*; *Lovesick* (Arcola Theatre); *Reimagining* (Almeida Theatre), *Last Easter* (Orange Tree Theatre); *Mission* (The Big House); *One Under* (Graeae

Theatre Company/Plymouth Drum/UK tour), *Superstar*, *Anything is Possible if You Think Hard Enough About It* (Southwark Playhouse); *New Views* (National Theatre), *Silence* (Mercury Colchester/UK tour); *Together, Not the Same* (Sadler's Wells); *Great Expectations* (Geffrey Museum); *The State of Things* (Brockley Jack Studio).

Mandy Demetriou Choreographer

Theatre includes: *Maria de Buenos Aires* (Buxton Festival); *Berlin to Broadway* (Copenhagen); *The Madras House* (Lyric Hammersmith); *The Woman Who Cooked Her Husband* (Nottingham Playhouse); *Glorious* (Duchess); *Pride and Prejudice*, *Emma*, *The Secret Diaries of Samuel Pepys* (Good Company); *The Diary of One Who Disappeared* (Arcola Theatre).

Opera includes: *Midsummer Nights Dream*, *Gentle Giant* (ROH Linbury Studio); *Capriccio* (Royal Opera House); *The Marriage of Firago* (English National Opera); *Hansel and Gretel* (Opera North); *Pagliacci*, *Cavalleria Rusticana*, *Lucia di Lammermoor*, *La fille du Régiment*, *Tl Trovatore* (Opera Holland Park); *Scoring a Century*, *Roméo et Juliette*, *Magic Flute*, *Albert Herring*, *La Rondine* (British Youth Opera); *Osud*, *Cherevishki* (Garsington Opera); *Mansfield Park* (Grange Festival); *Giulio Casare in Egitto* (Theatre An Der Wien, Vienna).

Film and television includes: *House of Elliot*, *Plotlands*, *Out of the Doll's House*, *Message for Posterity* (BBC); *Poldark* (HTV); *Goodnight Sweetheart* (Alamo Productions); *Lady Jane* (Paramount Pictures).

Brigitte Adela Assistant Director

Theatre includes: *Rose Tinted Glasses*, *Busstops* (National Theatre New Views); *Wakes* (The Bunker); *The Talk* (Rich Mix); *The Good Person of Szechwan* (Barons Court Theatre); *Collegiate* (Bread and Roses Theatre/Attenborough Arts Centre).

Brigitte Adela is a Creative Associate at Jermyn Street Theatre and Associate Maker at Coney.

Charlotte Thompson Dramaturg

Radio includes (as writer): *Stranger Faces* (BBC Radio 4); *Story of a Rude Gal* (BBC Radio 3).

Charlotte is a London based freelance dramaturg, writer, and teacher. She has worked for new writing companies such as Synergy Theatre Project and has a PhD in contemporary dramaturgy. She is currently a lecturer in playwriting, applied theatre and creative writing at Middlesex University.

Summer Keeling Stage Manager

For Jermyn Street Theatre: *Thrill Me: The Leopold and Loeb Story*.

Theatre includes: *Sugar Coat*, *Instructions for a Teenage Armageddon* (Southwark Playhouse); *The Boys Are Kissing*, *Til Death Do Us Part* (Theatre503); *The Grotto* (Drayton Arms Theatre); *The Light Trail*, *The Moors*, *Hand of God*, *21 Round for Christmas*, *Darling*, *Fever Pitch* (The Hope Theatre); *The Haunting of Susan A* (King's Head Theatre); *Ghosts of The Titanic* (Park Theatre); *Mario! A Super Musical* (The Cockpit).

Morgan Toole Assistant Stage Manager

For Jermyn Street Theatre: *Relatively Speaking*, *My Beautiful Future*.

Theatre includes: *Into the Woods* (The Playground Theatre); *Eugenius the Musical* (The Turbine Theatre); *Millennials* (The Other Palace).

a small theatre with big stories

WHO WE ARE

Jermyn Street Theatre is a unique theatre in the heart of the West End: a home to remarkable artists and plays, performed in the most intimate and welcoming of surroundings. World-class, household-name playwrights, directors and actors work here alongside people just taking their first steps in professional theatre. It is a crucible for multigenerational talent.

The programme includes outstanding new plays, rare revivals, new versions of European classics, and high-quality musicals, alongside one-off musical and literary events. We collaborate with theatres across the world, and our productions have transferred to the West End and Broadway. Recently, our pioneering online work and theatre-on-film has been enjoyed across the world.

A registered charity No. 1186940, Jermyn Street Theatre was founded in 1994 with no core funding from government or the Arts Council. Since then, the theatre has survived and thrived thanks to a mixture of earned income from box office sales and the generous support of individual patrons and trusts and foundations. In 2017, we became a producing theatre, the smallest in London's West End. Around 60% of our income comes from box office sales, and the rest in charitable support and private funding.

★★★★★
“ **Unerringly directed ... no one in this tiny theatre dared breathe.** ”

The Observer

From top: Jack Reitman in Thrill Me: The Leopold & Loeb Story, 2022; Jennifer Kirby in The Massive Tragedy of Madame Bovary, 2022. Photos by Steve Gregson.

★★★★★

OVER THE YEARS

1930s
During the 1930s, the basement of 16b Jermyn Street was home to the glamorous Monseigneur Restaurant and Club.

early 1990s
The staff changing rooms were transformed into a theatre by Howard Jameson and Penny Horner (who continue to serve as Chair of the Board and Executive Director today) in the early 1990s and

1994
Jermyn Street Theatre staged its first production in August 1994.

1995
Neil Marcus became the first Artistic Director in 1995 and secured Lottery funding for the venue; producer Chris Grady also made a major contribution to the theatre's development.

late 1990s
In 1995, HRH Princess Michael of Kent became the theatre's Patron and David Babani, subsequently the Artistic Director of the Menier Chocolate Factory, took over as Artistic Director until 2001. Later Artistic Directors included Gene David Kirk and Anthony Biggs.

2012
The theatre won the Stage Award for Fringe Theatre of the Year.

2017
Tom Littler restructured the theatre to become a full-time producing house.

2020
Our audiences and supporters helped us survive the damaging impacts of the Covid-19 lockdowns and we were able to produce a season of largely digital work, including the award-winning *15 Heroines* with Digital Theatre +.

2021
We won the Stage Award for Fringe Theatre of the Year for a second time. Artistic Director Tom Littler and Executive Director Penny Horner were recognised in The Stage 100.

2022
We won a Critics' Circle Award for *Exceptional Theatre-Making During Lockdown* and an OffWestEnd Award for our Artistic Director.

Stella Powell-Jones and David Doyle succeeded Tom Littler as Artistic Director and Executive Producer respectively, working alongside Executive Director Penny Horner to form a management team of three.

support us

> **I recently became a Patron of Jermyn Street Theatre, as I believe passionately in the work it is doing. It would be wonderful if you could contribute.**
> *Sir Michael Gambon*

Become a Friend of the theatre and enjoy a range of exclusive benefits. Join one of our four tiers of Friends with names inspired by *The Tempest* from just £50 a year.

Lifeboat Friends
From £4.50 a month

Our **Lifeboat Friends** are the heart of Jermyn Street Theatre. Their support keeps us going. Rewards include priority booking to ensure they can get the best seats in the house.

The Ariel Club
From £12.50 a month

Members of the **Ariel Club** enjoy exclusive access to the theatre and our team. As well as the priority booking and Friends Nights enjoyed by Lifeboat Friends, **Ariel Club** members also enjoy a range of other benefits.

The Miranda Club
From £45 a month

Members of the **Miranda Club** enjoy all the benefits of the Ariel Club, and they enjoy a closer relationship with the theatre.

The Director's Circle
From £250 a month

The Director's Circle is an exclusive inner circle of our biggest donors. They are invited to every press night and enjoy regular informal contact with our Artistic Director and team. They are the first to hear our plans and often act as a valuable sounding board. We are proud to call them our friends.

We only have 70 seats which makes attending our theatre a magical experience but even if we sell every seat, we still need to raise more funds.

Michael Gambon, Sinéad Cusack, Richard Griffiths, David Warner, Joely Richardson, Danny Lee Wynter, Rosalie Craig, Trevor Nunn, Adjoa Andoh, David Suchet, Tuppence Middleton, Martina Laird, Gemma Whelan, Eileen Atkins, Jimmy Akingbola and many more have starred at the theatre.

But even more importantly, hundreds of young actors and writers have started out here.

If you think you could help support our theatre, then please visit www.jermynstreettheatre.co.uk/friends/

Jermyn Street Theatre is a Registered Charity No. 1186940. 60% of our income comes from box office sales and the remaining 40% comes from charitable donations. That means we need your help.

our friends

The Ariel Club

Richard Alexander
David Barnard
Derek Baum
Martin Bishop
Dmitry Bosky
Katie Bradford
Nigel Britten
Christopher Brown
Donald Campbell
James Carroll
Ted Craig
Jeanette Culver
Shomit Dutta
Jill & Paul Dymock
Lucy Fleming
Anthony Gabriel
Carol Gallagher
Roger Gaynham
Paul Guinery
Debbie Guthrie
Diana Halfnight
Julie Harries
Eleanor Harvey
Andrew Hughes
Mark Jones
Margaret Karliner
David Lanch
Caroline Latham
Isabelle Laurent
Christine MacCallum
Keith Macdonald
Vivien Macmillan-Smith
Nicky Oliver
Sally Padovan
Kate & John Peck
Adrian Platt
Alexander Powell
Oliver Prenn
Martin Sanderson
Carolyn Shapiro
Nigel Silby
Philip Somervail
Robert Swift
Gary Trimby
George Warren
Lavinia Webb
Ann White
Ian Williams
John Wise

The Miranda Club

Anthony Ashplant
Gyles & Michèle
   Brandreth
Sylvia de Bertodano
Anthony Cardew
Robyn Durie
Richard Edgecliffe-Jones
Maureen Elton
Nora Franglen
Mary Godwin
Louise Greenberg
Ros & Alan Haigh
Nick Hern
Marta Kinally
Yvonne Koenig
Hilary King
Jane Mennie
Charles Paine
John & Terry Pearson
Iain Reid
Ros Shelley
Martin Shenfield
Carol Shephard-Blandy
Jenny Sheridan
Sir Bernard Silverman
Brian Smith
Frank Southern
Mark Tantam
Paul Taylor
Geraldine Terry
Brian & Esme Tyers

Director's Circle

Judith Burnley
Philip Carne MBE &
   Christine Carne
Jocelyn Abbey &
   Tom Carney
Colin Clark RIP
Lynette & Robert Craig
Gary Fethke
Flora Fraser
Robert & Pirjo Gardiner
Charles Glanville &
   James Hogan
Crawford & Mary Harris
Ros & Duncan McMillan
Leslie & Peter
   MacLeod-Miller
James L. Simon
Marjorie Simonds-Gooding
Peter Soros &
   Electra Toub
Fiona Stone
Melanie Vere Nicoll
Robert Westlake &
   Marit Mohn

Infamous

April De Angelis's plays include *Kerry Jackson* (National Theatre), *My Brilliant Friend* (adapted from Elena Ferrante's novels for Rose Theatre, Kingston, and NT), *House Party* (BBC4 and Headlong Theatre), *Gin Craze!*, a musical with Lucy Rivers (Royal & Derngate), *Extinct* (Stratford East), *Rune* (New Vic Theatre, Newcastle-under-Lyme), *The Village* (Stratford East), *Wild East* (Royal Court), *A Laughing Matter* (Out of Joint/NT/tour), *The Warwickshire Testimony* (RSC), *The Positive Hour* (Out of Joint/Hampstead/Old Vic; Sphinx), *Headstrong* (NT Shell Connections), *Playhouse Creatures* (Sphinx Theatre Company), *Hush* (Royal Court), *Soft Vengeance* (Graeae Theatre Company), *The Life and Times of Fanny Hill* (adapted from the James Cleland novel), *Ironmistress* (ReSisters Theatre Company), *Wuthering Heights* (adapted from Emily Brontë's novel for Birmingham Rep), *Jumpy* (Royal Court and Duke of York's Theatres), *Gastronauts* (Royal Court) and *After Electra* (Theatre Royal, Plymouth). Her work for BBC Radio includes *Visitants*, *The Outlander*, which won the Writers' Guild Award 1992, and *Cash Cows* for the *Woman's Hour* serial. For opera: *Flight* with composer Jonathan Dove (Glyndebourne), and the libretto for *Silent Twins* (Almeida).

APRIL DE ANGELIS

Infamous

faber

First published in 2023
by Faber and Faber Limited
The Bindery, 51 Hatton Garden,
London, EC1N 8HN

Typeset by Brighton Gray
Printed and bound in the UK by CPI Group (Ltd), Croydon CR0 4YY

April De Angelis is hereby identified as author
of this work in accordance with Section 77 of the
Copyright, Designs and Patents Act 1988

A CIP record for this book
is available from the British Library

978-0-571-38710-6

Printed and bound in the UK on FSC® certified paper in line with our continuing
commitment to ethical business practices, sustainability and the environment.
For further information see faber.co.uk/environmental-policy

2 4 6 8 10 9 7 5 3 1

Infamous was first performed at Jermyn Street Theatre, London, on 7 September 2023, with the following cast:

Emma Hamilton (1815) / Mrs Cadogan Caroline Quentin
Emma Hamilton (1798) / Horatia Nelson Rose Quentin
Vincenzo / Jacques Fournier Riad Ritchie

Writer April De Angelis
Director Michael Oakley
Designer Fotini Dimou
Lighting Designer Christopher Nairne
Composer and Sound Designer Beth Duke
Choreographer Mandy Demetriou
Assistant Director Brigitte Adela
Dramaturg Charlotte Thompson
Italian Language Consultant Gabriele Uboldi
Production Manager Lucy Mewis McKerrow
Stage Manager Summer Keeling
Assistant Stage Manager Morgan Toole
Photographer Steve Gregson
PR David Burns
Executive Producer David Doyle

Characters

PART ONE

Emma Hamilton
mid-twenties

Mrs Cadogan
her mother, late forties

Vincenzo
a young Italian manservant

PART TWO

Emma Hamilton
late forties

Horatia Nelson
fifteen

Jacques Fournier
young man

INFAMOUS

Part One

ONE

A room in Palazzo Sessa, Naples. 1798.
Mrs Cadogan, Emma's mother, enters. Emma is writing at a desk.

Mrs Cadogan I'm back! It's me. Fetch me wine. What a journey! I've been bounced across warring Europe in a mail coach. It's a miracle I'm all in one piece. Least I was last time I looked. Something could've fell off on the home stretch. Emma? Don't you want to hear my news?

Emma Not yet, listen to this. (*Reads.*) 'How shall I begin? What shall I say to you? 'Tis impossible I can write. I am delirious with joy! I am in a fever. God, what a victory! Never never has there been anything half so glorious. I fainted when I heard the joyful news and fell on my side and am hurt but what of that?' Do you think that's too much?

Mrs Cadogan Too much what?

Emma No, I think it's good. (*Continues to read.*) 'I should feel it a glory to die in such a cause except I would not like to die till I see and embrace the victor of the Nile.'

Mrs Cadogan What's wrong with shaking his hand?

Emma Mum! (*Reads.*) 'How shall I describe to you the transports of Queen Maria Carolina when she heard the news of your arrival? She fainted too – though did not injure herself as I did.'

Mrs Cadogan Injured?

Emma (*reads*) 'Sir William and I are preparing an apartment for you here in Palazzo Sessa. Oh brave Nelson oh Nelson Nelson. Now you are come to Naples you will be killed with kindness.

'For God's sake visit us here soon.'

Mrs Cadogan That's three Nelsons.

Emma 'Forever your grateful admiring adoring servant, Lady Emma Hamilton.'

Mrs Cadogan That's larding it. He's not a gentleman like Sir William.

Emma He doesn't have to be, he's famous. (*Reads.*) 'PS. My dress from head to foot is all à la Nelson, my earrings are anchors, in short we are be-Nelsoned all over. I am a living tribute to you and victory. Kiss this letter and send it back.'

Mrs Cadogan You can't say that, you're married.

Emma What's that got to do with it?

Mrs Cadogan And he's married too.

Emma Nelson saved our lives. Mine, yours, every man, woman, child in this city, in Italy, the whole of England. Snuck up on Bonaparte's fleet and kicked their French arses, otherwise they'd be here by now slaughtering us all in our beds. They'd cut off the Queen's head like they did her dear sister's, poor Marie Antoinette, they'd finish me off too because I'm the Queen's particular friend, probably string you up into the bargain.

Mrs Cadogan Why would they bother with me? A dogsbody? They'd wouldn't waste the rope.

Emma It's the least I can do to send a letter of appreciation.

Mrs Cadogan There's gratitude and there's giving it to him on a plate.

Emma It's politesse and keep your opinions to yourself. You don't know what we've been through. While you were on holiday our fate was hanging by a thread.

Mrs Cadogan It weren't an holiday. I was doing your bidding. You could have packed me a cushion. My bum's that red raw I'm afraid to look.

Emma kisses the letter.

Emma Sealed with a kiss.

Mrs Cadogan I know what you're about, luring him here like a spider.

Emma Sir William is the British Ambassador and I'm his wife. I'd be neglecting my duty if I was anything less than violently welcoming. Horatio Nelson is the name on everybody's lips and there isn't a woman in Naples who isn't longing to get her claws into him, but I'm going to get there first. Sir William must have a bit of his reflected glory.
    You're back just in time to do my hair.

Mrs Cadogan What for?

Emma It's one of my outstanding features and I need to be firing on all fronts.

Mrs Cadogan All fronts? You're only sending him a letter. He probably won't even open it.

Emma (*calls*) Vincenzo.

Mrs Cadogan I've been rattled around Europe in a carriage till I'm half-woman half-syllabub and for what if you don't want to hear what I've got to say?

Vincenzo enters.

Vincenzo Si, Lady Hamilton.

Mrs Cadogan Vino please, Vincenzo. The good stuff. I know the difference.

Emma He has more important things to do.
    Metti questo nelle mani del signor Nelson. Capite? Into his hands. Signor Nelson.

Emma hands him the letter.
    He doesn't move.

Velocemente! Get a move on.

Vincenzo Voi siete la donna più bella del mondo e.

Emma Vai vai.

Vincenzo Non riesco a dormire, non mangio, penso solo a voi – only of you I think.

Emma Do I care? Presto. Hurry. Go!

Mrs Cadogan What did he say?

Emma I'm too beautiful. He can't eat.

Vincenzo I write you. La poesia.

    He takes out a paper.

Emma Not a poem, please.

Vincenzo Tutto il giorno sospiro.
    D'amore muoio.

Emma Enough. (*To Mrs Cadogan.*) All day I sigh of love I die – awful. (*To Vincenzo.*) Sei una bestia.

Vincenzo Bella Emma.

Emma Vai vai, get going!

    He goes.

God. He's always staring at me – he leaves me little gifts.

Mrs Cadogan Like what?

Emma Little carved things – angels or creatures with arrows through them.

Mrs Cadogan Do you think he likes you?

Emma What do you think? – Would you fiddle around with wood unless you were totally smitten? He must be up half the night – he can hardly do his chores. He's infatuated.

Mrs Cadogan That letter was infatuated. You ought to be careful. It was a scandal when Sir William married you. They've only just stopped talking about it. And now you're risking another one. Kissing letters. All I'm saying is how many uncles would take on their nephew's cast-offs? You owe Sir William everything. The soft beds, the marble floors, the stars painted on the ceiling.

Emma He has as much reason to be grateful to me as I am to him. I put this place on the map with my soirées. People come here to eat my pineapples. I've even invented a whole new art form.

Mrs Cadogan Prancing around imitating them creatures you copied off his old vases?

Emma Goddesses, I think you'll find. And mythological entities. Goethe says I've dazzled the whole of Europe.

Mrs Cadogan Goethe who?

Emma Forget it.
  The togas I wear for my presentations are now all the rage in Rome, Paris and London, everyone is à la grecque in homage to mia, Emma. Pass me my diamond bracelet.

She does.

Mrs Cadogan It is beautiful. I never even had paste.

Emma But you get to see me wearing it, so that's some solace. Don't wait up for me.

Mrs Cadogan Why? Where are you going?

Emma The port, and I'm not accountable to you.

She gets up.

Mrs Cadogan I saw Little Emma.

Emma We're not talking about this now.

Mrs Cadogan That's why I went home, wasn't it? To see her settled after your Granny Sarah died.

Emma Don't. Do you want me to cry? My face will go puffy and I need to be striking.

Mrs Cadogan When my coach finally arrived at Bridlington she was waiting for me. Her little face all glowing, and she said, 'Where's Mummy?' And I said Mummy wanted to be here very much but she has a lot of engagements in Naples and couldn't get away but she sends kisses.

Emma What did she do? Was she very sad?

Mrs Cadogan Well you'd want her to be a little bit sad wouldn't you, because you wouldn't like a cold-hearted child?

Emma No, no. I'm sure she's not that, because I'm not cold-hearted.

Mrs Cadogan She understood. She sent you this.

She hands Emma a box.

Emma Oh, so pretty!

Mrs Cadogan I said, 'Did you decorate that all yourself?' and she said, 'Yes with silver filigree. It's quite hard, you have to curl it all up.' I could see she wanted to cry but she was being very brave. 'Mummy will write to you from Naples,' I said.

Emma Now *I'm* crying.

Mrs Cadogan 'Is Mummy upset with me?' she said. 'No,' I said, 'she's just busy and she's married a very important man, a diplomat. You'll understand when you're older.'

Emma How can I stand it? How did she look?

Mrs Cadogan Bright eyes. Curly hair. Just started losing her baby teeth. A proper doll.

Emma I can't think about it too much. My heart – I miss her every day.

Mrs Cadogan You'll have another child.

Emma Not unless it's an immaculate conception.

Mrs Cadogan You've worked miracles before.

Emma Sir William's seventy-three and his bagpipes have dried up.

Mrs Cadogan He might still be able to squeeze out the odd note?

Emma No. I'm going to ask him if we can have Little Emma sent over here. Why not?

Mrs Cadogan Sir William can't have a bastard love child wafting about. The British Ambassador! She's not even his bastard.

Emma I *will* ask him.

Mrs Cadogan He's only going to say no like he did before, and you don't want a reason to start hating him when we're so happy here. Our rooms have just been redecorated.

Emma Don't you want Little Emma here?

Mrs Cadogan Of course I do. More than anything. I'm her grandma. That's why I sorted everything so you don't need to worry about her. She won't go hungry. She'll be well looked after. She'll never have to take the path you took. Selling your tuppence on Brewer Street. You wouldn't like that for her, would you? The beadle and his wife are very upright people. We must count our lucky stars, not our falling tears.

Emma Am I a terrible mother?

Mrs Cadogan No, you're doing your best for her. You've made a sacrifice giving Little Emma up so you could live respectable here and send the money back. So don't go chucking it all away now, rushing down the harbour and making a show of yourself throwing yourself at an admiral.

Emma It's my duty! Anyone with a heart would be down there. A miracle happened and we should be thankful.

Mrs Cadogan You should listen to me. Don't I work hard for you? Don't I make all your fancy costumes with my own hands?

Emma You're with me because I'm a success. A great big huge shining diamond. And you get to live here in paradise with me. So don't tell me what to do.

Mrs Cadogan I may not have risen so high but I got us through. Don't forget.

Both While others ate straw you grew strong.

Mrs Cadogan Yes, because I put myself in the right place at the right time with Lord Hervey's under butler.

Emma And then you went off with him.

Mrs Cadogan I had to, love. He was our bread and butter. But we always kept in touch. Just like you and Little Emma. It's not a perfect world for mothers but we do the best we can.

Emma I'm not listening to this. Nelson is coming to our port. I'd be the most pathetic nothing if I wasn't down there to say hello on behalf of King George.

Mrs Cadogan Don't tempt fate.

Emma Listen to you, second-hand Sibyl.

Mrs Cadogan It's for your own good. I know you, Emma, you've got that gleam in your eye.

Emma Maybe I have a destiny.

Mrs Cadogan Destiny?

Emma Yes, did you ever think of that?

Mrs Cadogan No, because I don't know what it is.

Emma Sir William dug up a krater with the Three Fates on it, these old women spinning the thread of a life, and then one of them cuts it off.

All we have is how we act on what life throws at us.

Mrs Cadogan And life has thrown Nelson at you?

Emma Yes. It's only right he stays here. It shows all of Naples how important we are. That's our job.

I'm good at it.

I want the fires lit in the great hall. I want candles, wine, incense. I want my shawls laid out, oh and a musician.

Mrs Cadogan You're not doing your attitudes for him, are you?

Emma A hostess always has to be prepared.

Mrs Cadogan To be Aphrodite the goddess? You were born Amy Lyon, blacksmith's daughter.

Emma And I want you to do the bit parts.

Mrs Cadogan Me?

Emma I've been busy while you were away, researching. I've created a new one. Ever heard of a Bacchante?

Mrs Cadogan Is it a pipe of tobacco?

Emma No. She's a priestess, a follower of Bacchus, the god of wine and madness.

Mrs Cadogan Oh dear.

Emma Flowing hair, glinting eyes, translucent tunic. Tempted by a Satyr, know what that is?

Mrs Cadogan Not going to be good, is it?

Emma A male spirit with the ears and tail of a horse, hairy legs and a permanent hard-on.

Mrs Cadogan Oh my God.

Emma And that's what you're playing, since you've got the legs for it.

Mrs Cadogan Never.

Emma Here's your costume.

She chucks her a salami to use as a phallus.

Mrs Cadogan I'll never be able to eat that again.

Emma I'm the Bacchante.

She dances around provocatively.

Mrs Cadogan Emma!

Emma You're the Satyr, try and tempt me. Go on!

Mrs Cadogan Come over here, ducky.

Emma As a half-man half-horse with a stiffy.

Mrs Cadogan tries again.

Mrs Cadogan (*more gruffly*) Come over here, ducky.

Emma laughs.

You're not going to make me do it, are you?

Emma No, because I think even the victor of the Nile would be scared off if he saw that.

Mrs Cadogan Thank God.

Emma But don't ever tell me what to do again.
I'm leaving now. Don't wait up.

Emma goes to leave.

Mrs Cadogan Emma, there's something you don't know.

Emma What?

Mrs Cadogan Something important.

Emma This is just one of your wiles.

Mrs Cadogan No.

After I saw Little Emma, I went home to Neston, dropped in to lay flowers on Granny Sarah's grave. Got chatting to your Uncle Peter. He was talking about you, he said, 'How did she come out of you, because you're not beautiful?'

Emma You've got nice eyes.

Mrs Cadogan 'You're passable, but. Did you find her under a bush,' he said, 'like in the fairytale?' He was pissed. 'And now look,' he said, 'married to Lord Hamilton. She must have dirt on him.'

Emma He's my uncle but he's got a mind like a midden.

Mrs Cadogan 'Never known one like her for twisting men round her little finger,' he says.

Emma Why did you even bother listening to him? His brain's sozzled.

Mrs Cadogan He wants five hundred pounds.

Emma What?!

Mrs Cadogan I said I'd ask.

Emma He can go piss up a wonky wall.

Mrs Cadogan Can't you trust me and just give me the money?

Emma No. It's blackmail. He hasn't got anything – everyone knows I was a tart.

Mrs Cadogan It's not about you, it's about me.

Emma You?

Mrs Cadogan Yes.

Emma Why, what have you ever done?

Mrs Cadogan It's hard to put it into words.

Emma You don't usually have any trouble.

Mrs Cadogan Your father.

Emma Yes? My father?

Mrs Cadogan I wear these widow's weeds in his honour like any respectable woman would.

Emma Yes?

Mrs Cadogan You know I always said he died of a work-related injury.

Emma Horse kicked him in the head?

Mrs Cadogan It was me.

Emma You kicked him in the head?

Mrs Cadogan No.
   Not exactly.

Emma What are you saying?

Mrs Cadogan He was coming at me – drunk – he had a terrible temper – I panicked, picked up the nearest thing I could find, which was the ornamental cannonball your gran found on West Kirby beach and hit him on the head with it. He went down like a sack of potatoes.

Emma You didn't?

Mrs Cadogan Your Granny Sarah came in and said, 'What have you done?' I was crying. 'I think he's dead,' I said. 'You've only been married three weeks,' she goes, 'I know he was difficult but was this really necessary?' 'They'll hang me,' I said. She said, 'Just say he was drunk and he fell on it.' Which was quick thinking. So that's what happened. But it must have been playing on her mind, see, as she was dying and she went and confessed the whole thing to Uncle Peter and so now he wants a banker's note.

Emma You killed my father?

Mrs Cadogan What did your gran want to be bringing home a cannonball for? With most people it's shells.

Emma Didn't you love him?

Mrs Cadogan He was the lodger. He got very grimy in the smithy. One day I helped wash him down. One thing led to another and I got in the family way. The whole thing has made me so nervy. That's why I'm telling you, just live quietly here and don't got mixed up in anything global.

Uncle Peter's got a big mouth and he's going to have to be paid to keep it shut. Imagine how greedy he's gonna get if you get mixed up with a war hero?

The more famous you are, the more he's gonna press you for. And all the worry of it, I don't know if this poor frame of mine can bear it.

Emma It's your problem, not mine.

Mrs Cadogan Then I'm destroyed, Emma.

Emma You deserve it!

Mrs Cadogan We both are. Daughter of a murderess and wife of the British Ambassador to the Kingdom of Naples can't be the same person.

Emma God!

What use are you to me?

Telling me I can't have Little Emma here, harping on about respectability when all the time you were a common murderer.

Vincenzo enters.

Vincenzo Gli ho dato la lettera.

Emma You gave him the letter? Benissimo. Cosa ha fatto?

Vincenzo L'ha baciata.

Emma He kissed it?

Mrs Cadogan Vincenzo, there's a woman here in dire need of a glass of vino.

Vincenzo Ubriacona.

Mrs Cadogan What's he saying?

Emma You're a drunk.

Mrs Cadogan I'm Mrs Cadogan to him.

Vincenzo gets to his knees.

Vincenzo Abbiate pieta di me, Emma, vi supplico.

Mrs Cadogan What's he want now?

Emma Me to take pity on him.

Mrs Cadogan Tell him to get lost.

Vincenzo Vostro marito e un cagnaccio.

Emma My husband is an old dog.

Mrs Cadogan Cheeky sod.

Vincenzo Potreste permettervi molto di meglio.

Emma I could do much better.

Mrs Cadogan Give him a medal for persistence.

Emma Vai, vai e torna a lavorare.

She shoos him away.

Vincenzo Bellissima Emma.

He goes.

Mrs Cadogan Do you think he heard?

Emma You better leave.

Mrs Cadogan I've only just arrived. You don't really want me to go you're all I've got. I'll throw myself down Vesuvius.

Emma You'll have to get up there first.

Mrs Cadogan I'm telling you, Emma, you've gone Nelson mad and you should be careful.

Emma You don't get anywhere in life if you don't take risks.

Mrs Cadogan But you've got where you needed to get so you don't have to anymore. I'm sorry Little Emma can't be here. Don't send me away. We're good together. I've got nowhere to go. Please. Who'll do your hems?

Pause.

Emma I'll pay Uncle off.

Mrs Cadogan Thank you.

Emma I'll find a way to get the the money. Throw a big party, present my attitudes, Sir William will be so proud he won't notice how much I've spent.
I'll thrill them with my Bacchante.

She gives her Bacchante.

Seduce them with my Circe.

She gives her Circe.

Chill them with my Medea.

She grabs a knife and seems about to strike as she is suddenly filled with anger. Medea seems to take her over.

Mrs Cadogan Emma. It's me.

Emma stops.

Emma You did what you had to do to survive. I understand that. Like mother, like daughter.

Mrs Cadogan We'll have a quiet time in together. I can do some sewing. That lovely dress the Queen gave you needs letting out. Don't go down there to him, I'm begging you.

Emma Yes. All right.

She sits. Pause. Mrs Cadogan begins to sew. Emma gets up, looks out of the window.

It's so quiet. Everyone's gone down to the harbour.

Mrs Cadogan They like a party in Naples. Anywhere really.

Emma I sent him a letter though.

Mrs Cadogan I'm sure he got a pile of letters.

Emma But he will only have kissed mine.

Mrs Cadogan How do you know? He could have been hedging his bets. Kissed the lot.

Emma I was the one persuaded the Queen to let him supply his ships here before the battle. By rights, some of the glory is mine.

Mrs Cadogan holds up material.

Mrs Cadogan I love this colour.
Look at the old mountain. Puffing away like a witch's bumhole.

Emma Do you think if you hadn't caved my dad's head in we'd be sitting here now? In a palazzo?

Mrs Cadogan It's funny what the world throws at you.

Emma Sir William took me to visit Vesuvius.
We had to be pulled up by ropes. You sink to your knees and get covered in cinders, for every three steps forward you took two back, but at the top you can look down inside, see the beautiful liquid fire rumbling at its heart.

Mrs Cadogan What about that tourist got drawn closer and closer till the earth at the edge crumbled and he were thrown in head first?

Emma I can't wait up here with you, it's so boring.

Mrs Cadogan You could never sit still as a child!

Emma I'll creep down to the harbour.

Mrs Cadogan Emma?

Emma Keep to the shadows. Just get a peep of him. Come straight home. Someone else will sweep Nelson off to stay with them. There'll be plenty that will want to.

Emma goes.

Mrs Cadogan Be sure to come straight back. Emma? Emma!

TWO

Dawn.

Mrs Cadogan What happened?

Emma I don't know what came over me. I ran down to the harbour, and as he stepped off the ship in front of everybody I threw myself at his feet, flung my arms around him, cried, 'Oh God is it really you?' and fainted dead away.

Mrs Cadogan I expect that worked.

Emma Oh yes. Then we spent the night together.

Mrs Cadogan You never?

Emma He got into my carriage and we rode around the city. We talked. I told him everything. How I was a servant but couldn't stand it and ran away and went hungry and had to sell myself on the streets of Covent Garden, worked in Mother Kelly's brothel, was an erotic dancer at the Palace of Health, Pall Mall, actress's maid, Romney's muse, Fanshaw's mistress, Greville's mistress, Sir William's mistress, now wife.

Mrs Cadogan What did he say?

Emma He was really impressed. He thought I was amazing to have come so far and all under my own steam. He said if

I was a ship I'd be a great one. And then he told me all about himself. He's the fourth son of a vicar, he doesn't love his wife, she's a drip.

Mrs Cadogan You showed him the attitudes, didn't you?

Emma Just a few. We stopped the coach overlooking the bay I did them in the moonlight.

Mrs Cadogan I expect he liked them.

Emma Yes. He thought they were the most beautiful thing he'd ever seen.

Mrs Cadogan Sounds like it went well then.

Beat.

I drifted off to sleep waiting for you to come home, or at least I thought I was asleep but it was that halfway house and the clock struck and I looked up and saw the ghost again – an old woman in rags who says to me, 'Mother, Mother, it's me and I so want to come home.'

Emma That was a dream.

Such a busy day today. I'm taking Nelson to meet the Queen. Then when he's better we're having a great party for him, here.

Mrs Cadogan Is he sick?

Emma He's wounded.

He will need to be brought back to health, nursed and tended to.

Mrs Cadogan And you'll give him a good tending to.

Emma The man who is our only hope for salvation from Napoleon will be living under our roof. And I got him here. Half dead, true, but I'll bring him back to life. Pour all my strength into his poor broken body.

She puts on the attitude of the Sibyl.

Mrs Cadogan What are you doing, Emma?

Emma I'm the Sibyl.

I prophesy that from this dawn he will be so immensely famous that his name will go down in history and never be forgotten.

Mrs Cadogan And yours? I expect you want a bit of that fame too, don't you?

Emma Of course. It's the most powerful thing in the world. It can get you anything. It's like having a magic power. Remember that story you used to tell me when we were hungry, the magic tablecloth? And you'd just have to spread it and it would fill with fresh bread, meats, sweets. Everybody who comes near Nelson wants to touch his sleeve. Like he is the magic tablecloth. He can transform the lowliest thing, even a murderess's daughter, into something wonderful. Goodnight.

THREE

Two years later.
Emma, pregnant, is packing to leave.

Emma (*singing*)
    'Yet who alas can blame the lyre
    That pours a sound to Britons dear?
    The song shall future heroes fire,
    And bid them kindle as they hear,
    Through dangers seek the wreath of fame
    And bleed to gain a Nelson's name.'

Mrs Cadogan looks out of the window.

Mrs Cadogan I've got used to it now. Vesuvius.

Emma You couldn't stand it before.

Mrs Cadogan I know. And just as we have to leave forever I discover I like it after all. What's the word for that?

Emma Irony.

Mrs Cadogan Yes. I think she's a woman. Outside stone and still. Inside a heaving storm of molten fire which only erupts once a century. But when it does – watch out. Sir William's going to miss her too. He loves pootling about over there picking up his rocks.

Emma Are you going to help me pack or are you just going to stand staring out of the window like a lazy lazzaroni?

Mrs Cadogan I'm not a peasant. I should have a title too if you've got one.

Emma You have got a title. 'Housekeeper'.

Mrs Cadogan He was crying, Sir William, as they carried out his vases.

Emma He's lived here a long time.

Mrs Cadogan Says he's going to miss the lemon trees.

Emma He'll have to get used to English oaks.

Mrs Cadogan He's had a shock, that's all. I do feel sorry for him.
    Reading in a newspaper that he'd lost his job. That's not nice.

Emma You do know the ship's sailing today? We've got to get all this down to the harbour.

Mrs Cadogan You'll have to treat him very gently because he's been used to everyone calling him the Ambassador and running around after him, and now he's just plain Sir William with his collection of vases he dug up out of graves.

Emma Yes.

Mrs Cadogan Men aren't as good at disappointment as women. Because women have less expectations. We get shat on more and we get used to it. While a man like Sir

William's born into the lap of luxury. That's why he's upset. He's lost his job, his palace, his volcano, and . . .

Emma What?

Mrs Cadogan His wife's pregnant with another man's baby. He's bound to be a bit out of sorts.
  You have to be nicer to him, Emma. It's not every man that would consent to a mange à trois.

Emma Ménage.

Mrs Cadogan That's what I said. I sometimes think that Sir William should have married me. We get on. But he's twenty years older than me and that's not enough for some men, is it?

Emma You are talking about my husband.

Mrs Cadogan You don't love him.

Emma I do. In my way. I've always looked after him.

Mrs Cadogan We were so happy here. Then rumours of your mange have got back to Buckingham Palace and they say it's giving England a bad name.

Emma That's nothing to do with it. They don't want an ambassador who is too close to the Neapolitan royals. They think he puts their interest above his country's.

Mrs Cadogan Well he does. Cos your Queen Maria Carolina's best friend. Or that's what she pretends.

Emma It's not a pretence. I can tell if someone loves me or not. Pack that.

She throws her shawl.

We'll be all right. Sir William will sell his art. I've got my diamonds. Including the giant one Maria Carolina gave me for all my service to her. It's the size of a bollock.

31

Mrs Cadogan Are diamonds supposed to be foggy?

Emma It's worth a fortune. Anyway I won't need to sell it because Nelson's going to take care of us.

Mrs Cadogan Like he did before. Tried to drive the French out of Rome. Poke an angry bear in the ear and look what happened.

Emma How did the Neapolitan army, twice the size of the French and full of good-looking young men, fail?

Mrs Cadogan Good-looking young men have other things on their minds. You and Nelson cooked up that war between you for glory. Glory's gone to his head and you helped put it there with your anchor earrings. He whispers in your ear and you whisper in the Queen's and she tells the King what to do, just like in any marriage. Then it all goes tits up and we had to flee.

Emma It all turned out well in the end. We came back.

Mrs Cadogan And now we have to go again. I'm dizzy.

Emma Home to England – you should be happy!

Vincenzo comes in.

This is the last to go down to the carriage, Vincenzo.

He goes to pick up the trunk.

Mrs Cadogan He's got a face on him.

Emma He's probably heartbroken that I'm leaving. You never throw yourself at my feet now Vincenzo. Don't you love me anymore?

Mrs Cadogan I expect the whole palazzo will be in floods as they wave us off.

Vincenzo Saranno felici. They be happy. (*Pointing to the trunk.*) L'ultimo.

Emma Vincenzo, let's part as friends.
Whatever happened in the past we shouldn't let it spoil us.

She moves towards him. He makes no gesture towards her.

Are you still angry with me?

Vincenzo Nelson break treaty.

Emma The treaty was dishonourable, to let the rebels go free?

Vincenzo Eleonora de Fonseca. La poetessa.

Emma Vincenzo, she was a bad woman. She wrote terrible things about Maria Carolina in her republican newspaper. Called her a tyrant.

Vincenzo She beg you. You no help.

Emma The Queen wanted the women treated the same as the men, without pity.
When we fled the city the rebels took it over. It was chaos.

Mrs Cadogan Couldn't you just have let her off? You know what poets are like, they're sort of gentle pointless people.

Vincenzo She die, she cry, 'Viva la repubblica!' Donna molto coraggiosa.

Emma How brave she was is beside the point. Nelson worked hard to stamp out democracy, which is French so you should be grateful. Aren't you a patriot?

Vincenzo Nelson. Una sanguisuga.

Emma How dare you. He is not a leech.

Vincenzo Sul culo del re.

Emma And certainly not on the King's arse. I could have you arrested for that. You got your king and queen back, you should be happy.

Vincenzo has picked up the last trunk.

Vincenzo The republic will rise again. Then I happy.

Emma I saved you. Your mum came crying to me – 'Please get him taken off the list of traitors' – and I did.

Vincenzo Eleonora she have hard life, bad husband, jealous because she is famous poet, he beat her, she lose her baby.
  She want to learn everyone read poetry. But you no save her.

Mrs Cadogan It's always worse to see a woman hung, somehow.

Emma There was nothing I could do for her.

Vincenzo Goodbye, Emma.

Emma Take some wine from the cellar. For your family.

Vincenzo No, grazie.

Emma Have you no words for me?

He exits.

I'm cold suddenly. Where's my shawl?

Mrs Cadogan He's turned against you. Why did you have to get involved, Emma? We were safe here, but you had to meddle.I overheard the new ambassador. You're a scandal all over Europe.

Emma Dreary man! Such dreadful furniture.

Mrs Cadogan Pleasuring Nelson so he'd put your best friends back on the throne.

Emma No. I won't have that. We depart from Naples covered in glory.

Mrs Cadogan That's one word for it.

Emma We're going home, I'll be feted. The woman that loved Nelson back to life, the man who saved the kingdom of Naples and the world. I couldn't have done more. I'll be famous.

Mrs Cadogan Famous and respectable? Can a woman be both? The new ambassador said something else.

Emma Which I'm sure you're going to tell me.

Mrs Cadogan That you're destroying Nelson's good name. Like Circe, you'd put a spell on him.

Emma I'd never destroy his good name. I'd rather die first.

Mrs Cadogan He said however high up the slippery pole she's climbed, no one will ever forget she was born in a sty. Which is inaccurate. You were born on a truckle bed in the kitchen of your granny's cottage.

Emma No one will remember my past. I can hardly recall it myself. When they say Nelson, they'll say my name too, Emma. And then victory.
    The two of us together will be welcomed with open arms, the best known lovers in the world.

Mrs Cadogan You're just a dreamer. The best known lovers in the world? Until his wife shows up looking wronged. Until you get old like me and nobody wants you. Have a good look at me, cos this is going to be you one day. You're not one of those mythological creatures. You're flesh and blood, and you can suffer, get old. All my life's been a waste if I haven't taught you the one thing I know.

Emma What's that?

Mrs Cadogan What if something happens to Nelson? Half of him's missing already.

Emma Don't talk like that, you old fool. What do you know?

Beat.

The baby's kicking.

Mrs Cadogan Is he?

She puts her hand on Emma's stomach.

Oh yes.

Emma We are going to be so happy. I am going to give this baby all the love I couldn't give to Little Emma. I'll never be parted from him.

Mrs Cadogan I wanted a boy look what I got. The world is kinder to boys. But someone has to have girls, I suppose, otherwise –

Emma When we get home to England and he's born we're going to say that Nelson has adopted him as an orphan and I will be named his guardian.

Mrs Cadogan So he'll never know the truth.

Emma He'll be loved and loved and loved.

Mrs Cadogan Oh I suddenly feel so sad.

Emma At least I'll get to live with my child, watch them grow up, which is more that you ever did.

Mrs Cadogan That's cruel. I've always been on your side – where else can a mother be?

Beat.

One last look at the mountain. Goodbye, goodbye. Do you think it's sad we're going? Probably not. It's seen so much and it's made of rock.

She hurries out.

Emma What was the one thing you should have taught me?

But she has gone.
Emma is left alone for a minute.

Goodbye. It's all going to be wonderful.

She looks around. A sudden hesitation or doubt. She leaves.

Part Two

A barn in Calais. 1815.
  Mrs Cadogan now plays Emma.
  Emma now plays Horatia.

ONE

Horatia, a young woman, eighteen, sits in a bare room.
Sunlight streams in from an open doorway and windows.
The room is a rural outhouse of a farm building. There is
one mattress on the floor, or perhaps an old bed, an empty
wine bottle or two lie next to the bed, straw on the floor.
Horatia wears clogs. Apart from this, her dress shows that it
has seen finer days. She kneels on the floor scrubbing at a
petticoat with no soap in an old bucket. Her mouth is set.
After a bit she hears someone approach. She listens and
resumes her task. A snatch of a song from outside.

Emma (*singing, off*)
  'Yet who alas can blame the lyre
  That pours a sound to Britons dear?
  The song shall future heroes fire,
  And bid them kindle as they hear,
  Through dangers seek the wreath of fame
  And bleed to gain a Nelson's name.'

Horatia rolls her eyes. Shortly after, Emma enters, a
woman in her late forties who has seen better days too.
Her clothes, once fine, are bedraggled. She has a shawl
wrapped around her, now tatty. As she enters she appears
exhausted. She stands looking at Horatia, then pulls
herself together to make an entrance.

Emma Well.

Horatia scrubs.

It's me. Emma.

Horatia If I'd known you were coming I would have polished the silver.

She scrubs.

Emma It's a glorious day. Really, the town appeared quite picturesque and quaint.

Horatia (*still scrubbing*) What, Calais?

Emma The sun sparkling on the rooftops, the sea shimmering.
A cock crowed. A bell rang. A good omen, I always think. A woman said, 'Bonjour madame.' My spirits rose. A crowd of little children gathered about me, very charming and rural.

Horatia Did they throw things?

Emma No.

Horatia They usually do. Last week you got a black eye; a potato rocketing off your forehead.

Emma Well, a few of them threw things. But what do you expect? They're only children, they don't know any better. Such pretty children too, if a bit grubby. They don't mean anything by it.

Horatia They did. They usually call you 'la grosse sorcière anglaise'. The fat English witch.

Emma I do parler français, thank you.
I'm not that fat. By rights I should be skin and bone, just twigs rattling together under my gown, considering what I've been through.

Horatia You've got a long way to go before you get anywhere near resembling a twig. Not for years I shouldn't think.

She scrubs.

They call me things too.

Emma Do they?

Horatia The witch's daughter.

Emma Well, they've got that wrong. Although I do look upon you as if you were my own, Horatia, I owe that to your father. Still, if they call you names it diverts them from me. It's graceful to share.

Horatia I've learnt how to scrub anyway. Although I'm sure it works better with soap.

Emma You won't be scrubbing for long, dear. This is what one calls an unfortunate interlude. In years to come we'll look back and it'll be like it happened to someone else . . . someone we didn't even know and it'll be hard to feel sorry for . . .

Horatia So how did you get on?

Pause.

Emma?

Emma I just have to close my eyes, Horatia. I've never felt quite so terribly tired.
    On the way back the heat on the road was making it wobble.

Horatia Your visit. Was it successful?

Emma He's the very worst sort of Frenchman.
    One of those men one would like to stuff between one's breasts and watch kick for air.

Horatia winces.

Horatia So he turned you down. He wouldn't let you pawn your shawl?

Emma He said it was more hole than shawl. I told him it had a fashionable diaphanous weave.

Horatia What did he say?

Emma 'Get out.'

Horatia So what are we going to eat?

Emma Your father would be crying tears of pure outrage if he could see how we've been treated; thrown onto the dungheap of the enemy, abandoned by King and Country. I don't think this was what he had in mind when he bequeathed us to the nation. Also personally I paid six thousand pounds to various causes in the national interest. This is how we are rewarded. My heart is stamped on.

Horatia Anyway we'll continue to starve.

Pause.

Emma Listen to that bird singing.

They listen.

Do you think it feels happy?

Horatia Luckily it can eat worms.

She continues to scrub.

Emma It's important for us to remember that this isn't really us. We are above our circumstances.

Horatia So you keep saying.

Emma Think of the first time you met me.

Horatia I can't remember that far back. Probably there wasn't quite so much of you.
You must have been wearing something showy.

Emma My blue silk and my Nelson earrings, little gold anchors I had made to commemorate your father's victory in Egypt. I was very beautiful. I've lost count of the number of portraits I sat for . . .

Horatia Have to –

Emma When I first met your father he was much smaller than I expected, because you do expect a hero to be on the large side, but he was small with quite a lot of teeth missing, and he was also missing an eye and an arm and had a sort of hole in his head. Not the sort of man you expect to fall in love with.

We invited him to stay with us and I started to look after him, and then one day I thought, my God, I'll never be able to live without this person, how on earth did that happen.

Pause.

And now I do have to live without him. Every single day.

Horatia I'm just going to hang this out in the sun. Find a bush or something.

Horatia exits with the petticoat to hang it out to dry. While she does so Emma surreptitiously takes a bottle of wine out from beneath her shawl. She expertly removes the cork with her teeth and begins to drink. She hears Horatia entering, quickly replaces the cork and hides the bottle under the mattress.

Well, that's done.

Pause.

Can I take a look at your earrings?

Emma I think it's time you put all that behind you.

Horatia What?

Emma All this dwelling on the past. It's not healthy.

Horatia You do it.

Emma Me?

Horatia Constantly.

Emma What an exaggeration. I've always been a forward-looking individual.

Horatia The same stories drumming into my brain.

Emma When you get older you'll understand that the past has more appeal than the present.

Horatia Earrings.

She holds out her hand.

Emma I can't remember for the moment where I've put them.

Horatia What?

Emma I used to have servants for that sort of thing.

Pause.

Horatia Well, now I've got absolutely nothing to do.

Horatia begins to cry.

Emma What is it? What's the matter? Did something sting you? There are a lot of insects in France.

Horatia No.

Emma Well what is it, my love? Nothing ages a woman faster than tears.

Horatia Who cares? No one's going to see me here, we're cut off from everything in this hellhole of a place. Why are we here? There's no food and all you can do is sit there and drink.

Emma Drink? Don't be ridiculous.

Horatia There's a bottle under the mattress now. Isn't there?

Emma Well, yes, there is that bottle.

Horatia You still owed for the last twenty. He wasn't going to let you have more.

Till you paid what you owed.

Pause.

And now you've sold the very last thing – the earrings.

Emma What must you think of me –

Horatia You pawned my silver cup, the one my father gave me.

Emma You can blame the British Government. They owe me a pension for services rendered. I saved the life of the Neapolitan royal family.

Both The Queen sobbed her thanks in my arms.

Emma It seems a long time ago now. We'd fled Naples.

The little prince died in my arms that night – the worst moment of my life.

Until I got news of your father's death.

Horatia Of course you pawned them.

Emma It was theft. Then again, no French citizen wants earrings commemorating a battle they lost. I do wonder every day how I got from that fine lady you first met to this, and the thought of that is so unbearable that I –

She gets the bottle out and drinks.

Just can't face the day without wine.

But don't worry, darling, everything's going to be all right.

Horatia That, Emma, is the most ridiculous thing I've ever heard you say.

Emma I have talents, Horatia, that you would never believe. I don't boast about them. But trust me, I wasn't a mere decorative appendage to Sir William, I sang for my supper. We entertained on a grand scale and I was the pièce de résistance.

Horatia We're going to starve. I might as well lie here and never move again.

Emma My rise to fame began with my attitudes. Clad simply à la grecque, I performed with the sole aid of a shawl for the private guests of my late husband. Reports of my performances spread rapidly through the civilised world.

Horatia Like the plague.

Emma I was a little thinner then, but the art survives. Tonight, in the town hall, there's a summer banquet, various entertainments will be laid on and I intend to make an appearance.

Horatia If you think I'm letting you trot down to town naked except for a shawl you've got another think coming. They'll tie you to a stake and burn you.
    Then what'll happen to me? I'd rather hang myself with the wretched shawl than see you humiliate us both.

Emma I shall perform my attitudes. Researched with the aid of my late husband Sir William Hamilton from his lifetime's collection of antique vases and rare frescoes.

Horatia Oh God, you've gone mad.

Emma He was a fanatical collector of beautiful 'objets d'art', that's why when he saw me he couldn't resist. When that young man gets here I'm going to arrange it all.

Horatia What young man?

Emma The one I bumped into. The mayor's son.

Horatia You asked a man here?

Emma Don't worry, he's handsome.

Horatia What are you thinking, Emma? We can't have company.

Emma You were dying of boredom a moment ago.

Horatia We don't even have plates.

Emma Men don't really feel the same way about china as we do.

On board ship your father once ate maggoty bread off a wooden trencher.

Horatia I'm running away. It's too humiliating.

Emma He's a respectable young man, he's the mayor's son. The one we rent our rooms from.

Horatia We live in a barn.

Emma Don't be ridiculous. This isn't a barn. These are summer apartments.

Horatia For cows.

We live in a stinking barn!

A young man, Jacques, enters.

Jacques Bonjour, Madame Hamilton.

Emma Bonjour, monsieur. Say bonjour, Horatia.

Horatia Bonjour.

Emma Offer him a seat.

Horatia He probably just wants the rent.

Emma Nonsense. He's come because he likes ladies.

Horatia Emma.

Emma You should be mixing with people your own age. Young men especially, or you'll get out of practice and turn into a spinster.

Horatia Stop it. Please.

Emma Falling in love turns you from a girl into a woman. If you had a mother, that's what she'd want for you. Romance and a place in the world. I'm trying to help.

Horatia Emma!

Emma Asseyez-vous. S'il-vous-plaît.

Jacques Non merci.

Emma J'insiste. Je n'ai pas any other way.

He sits down.

Bon.

Emma Introduce yourself, Horatia.

Horatia Monsieur, je suis Mademoiselle Nelson.

Jacques Enchanté, mademoiselle. Je m'appelle Jacques Fournier.

Pause.

Emma Vin rouge?

Jacques Non merci.

Emma It is a trifle early.

Jacques Madame, mon père, Monsieur Fournier le maire, demande le paiement pour vos apartments.

Emma He wants the rent.

Horatia Oui. Je comprends.

Emma How much does he want?

Horatia I don't know, ask him what he usually charges the cows.

Jacques Je suis le messager. Je ne veux pas que vous partiez.

Horatia They're going to throw us out. We'll be destitute.

Emma He's being terribly nice about it. Tell him he'll get it and tell him it's a good thing he's come because I wanted to ask him something.

Horatia You tell him.

Emma It'll work better coming from you.

Horatia Elle est très heureuse que vous soyez arrive.

Emma I have a proposition for you. Une proposition.

Horatia That doesn't sound right in French.

Emma I am very skilled. Très supple.

Horatia That doesn't sound good either.

Emma Je perform mon attitudes cette nuit. Tonight.

Horatia No no.

Jacques Je ne comprends pas.

Emma I'll show him.

Horatia Please don't.

Emma Excusez-moi.

Horatia Oh God.

Emma I need a moment to prepare.

She exits.
Horatia and Jacques stand awkwardly.

Jacques English, no.

Horatia Je ne parle pas français très bien parce que I had to leave school.

Jacques Votre maman?

Horatia Non. Une amie.

Jacques Elle est très jolie.

Horatia But a bit fat.

Pause.

Elle est – um. Ici, c'est une prison.
She's keeping me here against my will.

Horatia indicates rattling the bars of a cage. The young man nods. Smiles. He doesn't understand.

Jacques Cette nuit. Le bal. Vous assistez?

Horatia Je ne sais pas. I may have other engagements. Engagée pour les autres.

Jacques Quel dommage.

Pause.

Horatia I haven't danced – been to a dance for a very long time . . . Oh, you're not going to understand that.

Jacques English. No.

Horatia But I do like dancing – and the music – when the music gets right inside you – as if it's streaming in your blood – and you stop thinking and you just dance –

Jacques Dance?

Horatia Dance. Yes.

She takes a few steps to show him. He nods.

And you feel free – like you're flying – and it's just so joyous and you never want it to stop – and of course there will be food there – a feast – God, I'm so hungry it's ridiculous. Hungry, you know? Like you could eat an actual raw cow.

She seems a bit dazed with hunger.
    The young man gets up and bows to Horatia as if he is inviting her to dance.

Jacques Dance?

For some reason, maybe because she is so hungry and therefore not herself, she accepts.
    They begin to dance when Emma bursts in.
    Emma drapes the shawl over her head and hunches up to create a sinister figure.

Emma The Sibyl at Cumae. Prophecy.

Horatia That's hideous.

Jacques is alarmed.

Jacques Mon Dieu.

Horatia You're scaring him.

Emma moves between each attitude seamlessly, like a sort of dance using her shawl. The Sibyl transforms into the sexually alluring –

Emma Circe delaying Odysseus from his voyage for a year. Seduction.

Horatia That's even worse.

Then with arms raised violently as if to strike –

Emma Medea: murderer of her children, slaughter.

She then sinks to a supplicating –

Mary Magdalene. Repentance.

Springs up, laughing, frenetic.

A Bacchante. Delicious abandon.

Falls again into an agonised posture with a concealed face.

Phaedra's shame. Illicit love. I think he liked that. And what's this next one?

Horatia I've no idea.

Emma Niobe, turning to rock for grief at the loss of her twelve children. Fortitude.

Horatia That's the last, isn't it?

Emma turns to stone. She wakes slowly to become –

Emma Ariadne. Deserted by her lover, Theseus, on Naxos. Abandonment.

Horatia Cheerful, aren't they?

She suddenly begins to wail.

Emma?

Emma is inconsolable.

Emma?!
   (*To Jacques.*) I'm sorry – she's quite emotional.

Jacques Est-ce qu'elle va bien?

Horatia Emma, for God's sake.

Emma pulls herself together.
Changes suddenly to joy.

Transformed by the kiss of a god to ecstasy.

Emma finishes.
The young man begins to applaud.

Emma You have to admit they're quite impressive.

Horatia Au revoir, monsieur. I think he's in shock.

Emma Ask him about tonight. If he wants me to perform.

Horatia He doesn't. Monsieur.

She shows him the door. Jacques begins to exit.

Jacques Madame, mademoiselle. Au revoir. That – was – unusual.

He exits.

Emma You foolish girl.

Horatia So humiliating!

Emma I could tell he likes you. I delayed my entrance deliberately.

Horatia He's a peasant.

Emma Take a look out of the window. His father owns every inch of land you can see and that lovely house in the town square.

Horatia What's that to me?

Emma And he owns our present lodgings.
  A woman has to seize her advantages, Horatia, while she can.

Horatia If you mean – that's disgusting!

Emma He just seemed a nice young man. You could do with a friend, couldn't you? I know I could.

  Pause.

Your father was very fond of my attitudes.

Horatia He was at sea a lot, he didn't get out much.

Emma That's very harsh, Horatia. Now I need a drink.
  I'm not good when reality buffets me. Feel like I'm at sea.
  And giant waves are getting ready to swallow me up.

  She takes a swig.

Horatia That's called inebriation.
  There'll be no need for you to disgrace yourself at the town hall because I shall be selling my petticoat.

  Emma has fortified herself with a few swigs.

Emma You can pay too much attention to what the world thinks. I've had the world at my feet.
  Your father and I only had to step out of doors, crowds would flock to us, cheer us. We were the most famous couple in the world. Every woman of fashion wanted to know what I wore. Sumptuous silks. But these hypocrites faded away – pointed their fingers at me.
  Affected disgust at our ménage à trois. If Sir William didn't mind, why should they?
  Eventually you came to live with us too.

Horatia I was too young to remember.

Emma Yes, after that. They spread vicious rumours about me. That as a young woman I'd danced naked on the table of Sir Henry Fanshaw's stag party.

Horatia And did you?

Emma Yes.

Horatia How repulsive. I don't want to know.

Emma It paid. I had to eat. Being hungry, as you are discovering, is no respecter of respectability. I said that without tripping up. I can't be as pissed as I thought. I shall be leaving for the town hall at six p.m.

Horatia We have nothing left but our dignity. Please try not to throw that overboard as well.

Emma Your father had a penchant for nautical terms. After eight brandies he always said, 'Flag's at half-mast.' He . . .

Horatia He's dead, Emma. Now we have to fend for ourselves. I shall be back shortly.

Emma With that rag – (*She gestures with the bottle in her hand to the petticoat.*) it's only worth a few sous.

Wine spills all over the petticoat.

Horatia Oh.

Emma What a waste.

Horatia It's ruined.

She rubs at the petticoat. Flings it away.

You stupid old woman.

Pause.

Sometimes I wonder if my father loved me.
    How could he if he left me to be looked after by you?

53

Emma He didn't know they'd give his pension to his brother. He willed it to come to us.

Pause.

Horatia I'm sorry, Emma. I shouldn't have said that. I was angry, and tired of all this I suppose.

Pause.

Emma?

Emma I'm feeling very peculiar.

Horatia How do you mean?

Emma Peculiar.

Horatia What, more peculiar than normal?

Emma Definitely. I actually can't get up.

She tries to and can't.

I don't think I'll be able to perform after all.

Horatia Thank God.

Emma You'll have to do it, Horatia.

Horatia Me!

Emma Yes. It's that or starve. And we can't starve, I promised your father.

Emma does a faint reprise of Niobe.

Fortitude.

She lies down.
Horatia looks at her, dismayed.

TWO

Dawn. Early light begins to filter into the room. Sounds of a very early morning. Emma lies on the bed, an empty wine bottle next to her. She stirs. She reaches for the bottle. Finds it empty.

Emma Bugger.

She closes her eyes as she hears Horatia enter. Horatia carries Emma's shawl as a bundle. She places it down on the floor and opens it out. On it are various foodstuffs: bread, cheese. She takes a roll and begins to gnaw it hungrily and diligently. Emma pretends to wake.

Horatia, is that you?

Horatia continues to eat hungrily.

Is that food? How wonderful. I couldn't eat a thing. I've been lying here half awake, half asleep, and really the strangest thoughts have been drifting in and out of my head. I was on a boat and the sea was raging beneath me and then I was in our garden in our old house and there was Sir William and your father and they were talking away about something and I thought they are looking pale I must feed them up and then I thought how silly of me because they're ghosts after all and then I thought about the last time Nelson left us for Trafalgar he ran back up to say goodbye to you four times because he loved you so dearly and he hated to say goodbye you just slept through it I think you weren't an oversensitive child he hated to leave you and he hated to leave me and in the end I had to tell him to go and he said, 'Brave Emma, if there were more Emmas there would be more Nelsons,' and then I wondered did he have some kind of presentiment that he was never coming back.

Pause.

And then I was on a boat again drifting and I thought
I know what I am I must be an attitude but I couldn't think
which one –

Horatia Drunkenness.

Emma Probably. That was very witty, Horatia. And
I thought about you and how you were down at the town
hall performing your attitudes and I felt very proud of you
and proud that I'd taught you something at least. My, you
are hungry.

Horatia continues to eat.

So, how did it go?

Horatia Marvellously. I rushed out in front of the good
people of Calais, whipped out my shawl and performed a
series of antique poses that left them breathless and gasping
for knowledge of classical Greece. At least for a brief pause
they had been forced to think about something other than
cheese.

Emma Cheese? What has cheese got to do with it?

Horatia It was the annual cheese producers' dinner dance.
Actually their cheese is rather marvellous.

Emma Cheese or no cheese, I'm glad it went well.

Horatia It didn't go well. It didn't go at all.

Emma No?

Horatia No.

Emma They were too busy guzzling?

Horatia Yes, they were too busy guzzling and also I was
outside the building.

Emma Outside?

Horatia Yes, looking in through the window until someone
shooed me off.

Emma Shooed you off? Do they know whose daughter you are?

Horatia Apparently not. Although I don't think that would have helped matters, do you?

Considering my father was responsible for the most ignominious naval defeat in their history.

Emma Why didn't you force your way in?

Horatia Force my way in? I looked through the window and saw people who were dressed in clean, fashionable clothes. They were conversing together in a civilised manner. Some were laughing. There was a girl the same age as me who looked like a girl I used to go to school with and she was glowing and laughing too, and I thought, what am I doing standing out here in clogs? I'm not going to go out in front of those people and be humiliated, like singing for my supper.

That's the sort of thing you have done, or worse, but I will not sink to that.

I am not like you. I don't want to become like you. My father was Lord Horatio Nelson, and you, from what I can make out, are the pushy daughter of a Cheshire blacksmith who whored her way to the top.

Emma Lovely countryside, I miss it.

Horatia Later one of the servants took pity on me and gave me some scraps. Delicious.

Emma What about the young gentleman who was here earlier? Did you get the chance to renew your acquaintance?

Horatia My father was killed by a Frenchman. I don't think he'd appreciate my cultivating one.

Emma You're a nice girl, Horatia, but you can be a little stuffy.

Horatia What I don't understand is how my relatives haven't tried to do anything for me. How they've left me here in the land of the enemy to rot.

Emma I understand perfectly.

Horatia Why?

Emma They're bastards.

Horatia I'm surprised they haven't written.

Emma Yes.

Horatia pulls out a letter which is tucked into her clothes. She reads.

Horatia 'Dear Lady Hamilton, we are sorry to hear that you have had to leave England so precipitously to escape your creditors and we were saddened to learn of your spell in the King's Bench prison and hope it has not had too marked an effect on Horatia . . .'

Horatia breaks off here.

I'll never forget the rats.

She continues.

'Debt is an iniquitous thing. Having . . .'

She breaks off again.

I don't know why I'm reading this. I know it by heart.

She puts the letter down.

'Having left England for France and taken Horatia from her country and its protection from all she loves and knows, we advise you in the strongest possible terms to return her to her nearest relatives, where she will continue to receive the education and respect due to a lady of her connections and advantages. I am sure you will see the wisdom in this arrangement. I remain your faithful, et cetera, et cetera.
      'William, Earl Nelson.'
That's my uncle.

Emma You do surprise me, Horatia, you must have been rifling through my personal correspondence.

Horatia In the circumstances I feel it was justified.

Emma It's a pity they didn't see the wisdom in paying a few of our debts. Then we might not have had to flee so precipitously.

Horatia Perhaps they didn't want to throw good money after bad.

Emma It's true, I'm an appalling creature, but on the other hand I'm sure I don't deserve my present circumstances.

Horatia I know I don't.

Emma People have short memories.
    There would have been no Nelson to win Trafalgar if I hadn't nursed him back to health. These hands changed history. Fetch me another bottle.

Horatia Before breakfast? No.

Emma He was skin and bone and empty and sad. I made him come back to life. 'Santa Emma' he called me. He always carried my likeness.

Horatia Why have you kept me with you?

Emma Why?

Horatia Yes.

Pause.

You're a selfish woman, Emma. You wanted me because I'm a part of him. Well, he's gone and you have to let me go. I want to live with my nearest relatives. Who happen to live in civilisation and not a shed. It's cruel of you to keep me here. My father entrusted you to care for me and you've failed to carry out his orders. They'd shoot you in the Navy for that.

Emma I've run out of red wine. No one should ever run out of red wine.

Horatia I want to go. You have to let me go.

59

Emma But I'll be on my own.

Horatia I can't stay here. Living like an animal. I'm the daughter of a national hero.

Emma I'm not good on my own. I'm too used to being the centre of attention.
  When I hosted your father's fortieth birthday party in Naples we had seventeen hundred guests.

Horatia I'm walking down to the port and getting on the first English boat. I'll tell the captain who I am – I'm sure they'll take me.

Emma Very well, but before you go I hope you'll tidy up a little. In case I receive any guests.

Horatia Yes, Emma.

Emma And pass me my shawl.

  Horatia does.

Goodbye.

Horatia There's some food here and when I get to England I'll send you some money if I can, but you must promise me not to spend it on drink.

Emma I can't promise anything of the kind.

Horatia Very well. I'll send you some anyway I suppose. Goodbye, Emma.

  She kissses her.

Take care. For your own good, please don't attempt to perform your attitudes.

Emma I don't want a lecture, Horatia, I'm dying.

Horatia I don't think you are, Emma. You're just trying to keep me here.

  Pause. Emma turns her face to the wall.

Emma I can't tell you why I kept you with me. It would be breaking a promise, and unlike the British Government I always keep my word.

Horatia You thought people wouldn't desert you if you kept me with you. Well, you were wrong. Or was there another reason, Emma?

Emma Your father always said I should look on you, his adopted daughter, as if you were my own. He was always looking after people. That's why his sailors liked him. He hoped I would be a matronly influence on you.

Horatia Well, that worked. Is there something you haven't told me, Emma? Because I've always wondered.

Emma sighs.

Who my mother could be. You don't have to be a genius to work out the dates.

Emma Sometimes I get angry with your father, leaving us to the nation! It's not a thing to be relied on.

Pause.

Horatia Emma?

Pause.

Emma?

Horatia goes closer. She looks at Emma, who has died.

Oh no oh no no no.

She stands for a moment, not knowing what to do.

THREE

Weeks later. The same room.
  Horatia enters. She is now well dressed.

Horatia I can smell animals.

  Jacques enters.

Des animaux. Animals.

  She sniffs.

Jacques Animals.

Horatia Yes.
  There are holes in the roof. I'd forgotten that.

  She points.

Jacques The ceiling.

Horatia Yes. La pluie.

Jacques The rain.

Horatia Yes. I'm surprised we didn't catch our death – Well –

  Pause. He points to the bed.

Jacques The bed.

Horatia Yes. The bed. Très bien. And thank you for coming here with me today.

Jacques My pleasure.

Horatia Your family has been so kind to me. I don't suppose I'll ever be able to repay you.

Jacques Too fast.

Horatia Merci beaucoup à votre famille pour moi. Or something.

Jacques Ah. Thank you.

Horatia I'm going home tomorrow – my respectable relatives stepped up to post – I'll miss you – all of you.
Je suis triste.

Jacques Sad. Yes.

He sees Emma's shawl. He picks it up.

For you. Her – thing.

Horatia Yes, it is a bit of a thing.

Jacques Qu'est-ce que c'est?

Horatia Shawl.

Jacques Shawl. Shawl.

She takes it.

Horatia I think it's made me a bit strange.
Living here. And then the death.
And having no one and running down to the village.
I think people don't know what they would do.
Until it happens to them.

Jacques shakes his head; it is all too fast. She holds up the shawl.

I just wanted a memento. I have nothing of hers, literally nothing.

Jacques shrugs.

You're not getting a word of this, are you?
I think you like me a bit, don't you?

Jacques What?

Horatia It's quite mutual. Emma would have done something about it.
But the thing is, I'm not like Emma. To tell the truth I'm much too stuffy. This shawl.
It's tasteless and full of holes. It's perfect.

Jacques Perfect?

Horatia Yes. It's very Emma.
  You really have nice eyes.

Jacques I don't understand.

Horatia Just as well. Really. I think. We should go. Emma.

Jacques Yes, Emma.

Horatia I'm wondering what she would have done now?
  It was like she was never here. She's just vanished. Except
in my head.
  Sorry, I'm rambling. I know what she would have done,
she would have kissed you.

Jacques You want to go?

Horatia Yes. I got what I came for.

Jacques Shawl.

Horatia That's not true. I haven't. But you'll never know
that. I'll tell you something else too. Emma was my mother.
  It's all clear to me now. Why she kept me with her. What
she promised my father she'd never tell. I just couldn't
admit to it before. I don't know why. Too stuffy, I suppose.
  She was my mother, ma mère.

Jacques Yes, of course.

  Pause.

Horatia You knew?

Jacques Yes. Because you argue.

Horatia Yes.

Jacques And you both are beautiful.

Horatia What a pity – you know – we never –
  Fortitude, fortitude.

She makes the attitude with the dirty shawl.
    Then she tries something else.
    The Bacchante.
    He applauds.
    For a moment it's as if they are going to kiss.

I'm not Emma.

She moves away.
    The young man laughs.
    She takes one look at the shawl and bundles it away.

I think I'll stick with fortitude. I've got a long journey.

He opens the door for her. They leave together.
    End of play.